SH*T DOESN'T JUST HAPPEN!!

a handbook of
Supersoul Spirituality

IAN LAWTON

Rational Spirituality Press **RSP**

First published in 2016 by Rational Spirituality Press.
All enquiries to be directed to www.rspress.org.

A CIP catalogue record for this title is
available from the British Library.

ISBN 978-0-9928163-2-2

Cover design by Ian Lawton.
Author photograph by Simon Howson-Green.

*this book is dedicated to
anyone who is suffering*

*because this illusion is
so very persuasive*

*who has forgotten they're
an actor in a grand play*

*making up their own
script as they go along*

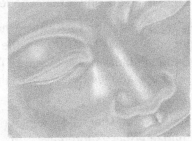

preface

SH*T DOESN'T JUST HAPPEN!!

One night not long after I started writing this book I took a late-night stroll along the beach. In my headphones I was listening to a recording of a fellow researcher talking about the neural pathways in the brain, how they create our perception of 'reality', and how we can retrain them to create any set of experiences we want.

After an hour or so I arrived home in pensive mood. As I walked through the hallway of the Georgian block of flats where I live, I glanced in the huge antique mirror... and that's when it hit me.

For several years I'd been writing about the fundamental supremacy of the 'law of attraction', particularly in my books *The Power of You* and *What Jesus Was Really Saying*. Indeed even before this I'd realised that the traditional reincarnatory worldview I'd previously supported didn't dovetail properly with this supremacy at all. So much so that while researching *Supersoul*, the first volume in this series, I'd spent many months – and almost exhausted my limited brain power – working on a completely revised model of soul consciousness that does fully allow for this supremacy.

SH*T DOESN'T JUST HAPPEN!!

I had also attempted to bring all this theory to bear on my own life. But now, for the first time, I realised there'd been a part of me that still hadn't been sure. Hence the poor sales of these books, and my reluctance to get out and talk about them – something I'd tried to dismiss with excuses. Indeed for a short time I'd even managed to attract a partner who clearly mirrored this uncertainty back to me by repeatedly questioning my beliefs: "If you're creating all this and you want your books to be selling, how come they're not?"

But now, finally, something I'd written about actually happened to me. I stared at my reflection in the mirror and, as a deep sense of joy and relief brought tears welling up, I spoke aloud: "I'm *not* mad. I'm *not* talking nonsense. This stuff is actually *real!*"

Finally, belief had become knowing.

Ian Lawton
March 2016

My sincere thanks go to Janet Treloar, Ken Huggins and Victoria Moore for taking the time and trouble to read through the manuscript and

SH*T DOESN'T JUST HAPPEN!!

provide invaluable feedback.

Please also note that this book is intended as a simple introduction to the concepts involved in what I've come to call 'Supersoul Spirituality'. It contains multiple footnotes indicating where further discussion of the relevant research and evidence, and more complex analysis, can be found. They mainly refer to the more detailed research books that make up the first three volumes of this series: 'Supersoul', 'The Power of You' and 'Afterlife'.

you're not a victim, ever,
of anyone or anything...
you're always in
the driving seat

SH*T DOESN'T JUST HAPPEN!!

When I was a thrusting young London-based software salesman in the materially obsessed Thatcherite 1980s, I had no sense of spirituality whatsoever. But I did manage to work out one very important thing that has stayed with me ever since.

People used to say to me, 'Ooh, software sales, that must be a really pressurised job. It must be terribly stressful.' But I would always respond, 'No, it's not actually. It's pretty easy.' Why was that?

Once I'd established myself the managers in the company knew I could bring in the business, so they just let me get on with it. New sales directors and managers would come and go, each one keen to stamp their imprint on the team with some new initiative concerning the number of cold calls and appointments we had to make each week – and the poor guys who weren't very skilled, or weren't lucky enough to have as good a set of customers as me, suffered serious stress. But as I said, I was just left alone to get on with it.

So it was I came to realise that stress doesn't stem from working hard, but from feeling we're *not in control*. From being constantly pressurised by a boss, a spouse, a family member or a combination of all of these. Or, more generally, from just feeling that there's too much to do, that there's never enough time, that everything is crowding in on us and spiralling out of control.

More recently I've come to realise that a corollary of not feeling in control is a tendency to see ourselves as a victim. As soon as we blame something undesirable in our life on our boss, our spouse, a family member or a friend, we're giving away our control over that situation and placing ourselves at the mercy of someone or something else. This stress is pretty much guaranteed to lead to pain and suffering.

By contrast it's very hard to suffer when we feel we're in control. We can be as busy as we like, whether it's with work, raising a family, following a sporting dream or whatever. But if we enjoy what we're doing, we know we're doing it because it's what we want to do and no-one else is making us do it, and we enjoy the benefits that derive from it – whether financial or otherwise – we don't feel stressed. We might feel tired on a regular basis, but not stressed, and we're certainly not in pain or suffering. Quite the opposite.

It naturally follows that if we take full responsibility for everything we experience in our life, and never allow ourselves to sink into victim mode by blaming things on anyone or anything else, much of our suffering will vanish. So taking responsibility for our own lives isn't a burden to be avoided – it's actually the ultimate in self empowerment.

But it's not only by blaming other people that we avoid taking responsibility. We can do it in other, more subtle ways. Indeed the bulk of the human race has been doing it for many millennia – ever since we first started to wonder why we're here, and to imbue all manner of gods and prophets with power over our destinies, both individual and collective.

More recently the influx of Eastern thought into the Western world has produced other, even subtler ways in which we can avoid taking responsibility. Concepts such as karma from a past life, for example, can lead some spiritual seekers to assume a certain sense of inevitability to their suffering – if they believe they're somehow paying the price for past misdemeanours.

The same *can* be true of the more modern and increasingly popular concept that we actually plan the challenges of our own lives in advance, while in soul form. When I was first introduced to this idea I thought it was wonderfully empowering. After all, the notion that we might actively *choose* to be differently abled, for example, in order to challenge ourselves and to grow from a soul perspective, is far more empowering than the idea that such people are paying some sort of karmic price – or, worse still, at the mercy of a capricious God. But is it really quite so simple?

Of course we all have our own unique experiences and I can't definitively speak for anyone else. But I suspect mine might shed some useful light on this whole issue.

Some years back I went through an extremely difficult couple of years. I won't go into detail here, not least because it's all recorded in a little book called *The Gift*. Suffice to say that I lost my job, I had little money, I ended up living in a van,

SH*T DOESN'T JUST HAPPEN!!

I lost most of my friends, my books weren't selling well at all, and in the end I lost my girlfriend too.

I had dismissed traditional concepts of karmic debt long before this. But I did repeatedly allow myself to ponder whether all my suffering might not be the result of a life plan where I'd set myself some extremely harsh challenges. My 'spiritual ego' almost wore it as a badge of honour that I was putting myself through so much.

Then, finally, I woke up. I realised that all this was just avoidance of taking responsibility for what I myself was creating in the here and now. Finally I understood that, despite all my genuine and various efforts to pull myself out of the black hole, I'd simply allowed myself to become a victim again and again. At that point I vowed 'never again', took back control and began to re-emerge into the light.

I am not suggesting for one moment that all people who believe in concepts such as karma or life planning use them as ways of avoiding responsibility. But I know I did, and I suspect I'm not alone. I know that when I first started writing purely spiritual books, and used to attend various mind-body-spirit fairs and similar gatherings, many people would approach me and proudly reveal, 'I'm sure I'm on my last life, I've suffered *so* much in this one, I must be paying off *all* my past karma in one go.' It pains me to admit how I judged them at the time. Little did I guess that within a few more years I'd be attempting to wear a not-entirely-dissimilar badge of honour.

My research in recent years has taken me down a very different path. That is not to say that my earlier work in the *Books of the Soul* series is now completely invalidated, because it still represents a useful introduction to a spiritual worldview based on rationality and evidence – hence the term I coined, 'Rational Spirituality'. But a number of pieces of evidence have more recently come together to suggest that our traditional view of reincarnation as a series of lives one after the other needs a major overhaul – as indeed does our whole model of soul consciousness.

We will talk about the evidence that underpins this new 'Supersoul Spirituality' in the next few chapters. But the other thing it reveals is that – at least once we reach adulthood – each of us is creating or manifesting all aspects of our experience of this reality via our own thoughts, beliefs, intentions and conditioning. No one else. Just us.

This assertion of the primacy of the so-called 'law of attraction' will be highly contentious for some people, so can I provide any initial backing for it? The first thing I would point out is that, from a scientific point of view, research into the linkages between mind and matter has been expanding rapidly for several decades and is producing significant results. Leading the charge is former medical school professor and research scientist Dr Bruce Lipton, whose *Biology of Belief* is the seminal work in this area.

To support this, for several decades now pioneering studies have been producing a huge amount of evidence to support the notion of the 'placebo effect'. For example, people with back or shoulder pain have had operations that completely mirrored the real thing except once the surgeons were inside the body they did nothing – yet significant numbers of patients subsequently reported a lessening or complete cessation of pain.

On a more purely mental level, track cyclists were given a new, supposedly performance-enhancing pill made only from cornflower, and every single one improved their times. Students suffering from relationship heartbreak were given a supposedly analgesic nasal spray that contained a weak saline solution, and a significant number reported feeling better about their ex-partner.

Perhaps best of all, a large, recent UK study saw 117 people in Blackpool, who had suffered severe back pain often for more than a decade, take a 'new' painkiller. Crucial was that they believed in the authenticity of the whole programme, so the researchers set up a pretend medical clinic with real doctors and proper consultations, the pills needed to look authentic, the bottle had all the usual stuff on the label and so on. After three weeks more than half felt their pain had lessened considerably or completely gone. Best of all the effect continued in many of them even after they were told they'd only taken a placebo.

This is now providing us with proper, scientific

evidence of the power of mind over matter. Or, to put it another way, of how our thoughts and beliefs condition our experience.

Apart from this there's also plenty of everyday evidence that we can deliberately create desirable outcomes in our life. For example, it's now pretty much essential for a top sportsperson to employ a psychologist to help them win. This is because it's commonly understood that repeatedly visualising a winning outcome and behaving as if it's a foregone conclusion – even one that's *already happened* – will massively increase the chances of that outcome being realised.

So it would appear that as human beings we've been given huge power to influence, indeed create, our experience of this plane. Nevertheless, one oft-touted objection is whether this power is genuinely available to everyone, or whether those faced with less favourable life circumstances are somewhat hampered. This question has complexities that we'll return to in a later chapter but for now, from a purely logical point of view, why would anyone or anything design a system that gives some people this power but deprives others?

SH*T DOESN'T JUST HAPPEN!!

Another key question that arises is this:

If we accept that it's possible to create desirable outcomes in our life, why would we then insist on blaming something or someone else for our less desirable experiences? Where would be the logic in that?

I contend that it makes most sense to accept that as adults we're creating the *entirety* of our experience. The only major rider to this is that the circumstances of our birth in terms of our sex, location, parents, psychological and physical traits and so on will have a huge potential impact on our lives, something we'll discuss in more detail later.

In conjunction with this I contend that we can replace the traditional reincarnatory model of soul consciousness with an entirely new, matrix-style one based on simultaneous lives that not only better fits the available evidence but also, perhaps for the first time, is entirely compatible with this primacy of the law of attraction.

So how do we manage to attract these *undesirable* outcomes that we *don't* consciously want at all? The problem is that much of our creative process is driven by a *subconscious* that can hold very different views from those of our conscious mind.

For example, let's say someone loses their job because their company goes bankrupt. On the face of it they'd say, "There's no way I *caused* that to happen, it was completely outside of my control!" But actually, when we look deeper, we'll almost certainly find that some inner motivation was at play in their own psyche. What is more it would be something entirely different for each person made redundant – from, for example, a deep insecurity about their future, to a core belief that they don't deserve prosperity, to an inner desire to change their path in life. *Something* individual to each person will have caused them to have that experience.

In fact a major challenge for each of us as human beings is to lay bare, and then heal and transform, the blockages and unhelpful beliefs that reside in our subconscious – which tend to sabotage our experience of what was always intended to be a joyful and abundant life. Only then can our true creative potential blossom and thrive.

*to create the life you want,
learn to understand that you're
already creating the life you're
having... all of it, all the time,
in every moment, no exceptions*

SH*T DOESN'T JUST HAPPEN!!

We have just seen that we create our own reality via the law of attraction. We do this not just with our proactive thoughts and intentions, but also with our underlying beliefs, preconceptions and attitudes – indeed via everything that forms part of our psychological, mental and emotional make up, both conscious and subconscious.

But the key point we now need to take on board is that we're doing this literally *every* moment, at least while we're awake. Creating our own reality is not an optional extra we can choose to add to our experience just when we feel like it. We never have a single moment off from creating. It is an automatic process.

That is why it's so important to understand how it really works. Because once we understand that we can start to focus on maximising the amount of time spent on creating experiences we do want, and minimising the amount of time spent on creating those we don't. It is all about where we choose to place our *focus*.

In a later chapter we'll look at the tried and tested techniques that optimise our efforts at conscious, deliberate creation of outcomes we desire. But first we need to recognise the ways in which our subconscious might be sabotaging these efforts. Some of the more popular books on this topic tend to avoid this crucial area, leaving people baffled when all their efforts to direct their life in a more positive way result in failure – and they end up feeling worse than ever. With all the love in the world we can't help but see this as seriously irresponsible and unhelpful to people who are sometimes extremely vulnerable.

This is not intended to be a detailed self-help manual, but there are a few key pieces of advice that are essential to our understanding of the creative process.

We all know how the mind loves to chatter away to itself. Indeed the voice in our head is always looking for something to worry about. It may be that this originates in a survival mechanism from earlier chapters in human history, but for most of us in the modern world the threats to our safety and survival are relatively few. What is more from a reality-creation perspective this endless chatter or noise, which nearly always concentrates on undesirable situations that have occurred in the past or might occur in the future, is seriously unhelpful. Yet we become so used to it that often we simply don't notice it at all. It becomes like the background 'mood music' playing in a lift.

So the first key skill we should aim to develop is to train our 'observer self' to monitor our thoughts, to catch the less desirable ones before they can take hold, and to replace them with more desirable ones. Those that are less desirable are often called our *limiting* thoughts and beliefs. In other words, if deep down we believe we're unworthy of love, friendship, success or whatever then, even if *consciously* we might be desperate to manifest these things in our life, we'll continue to create a reality in which they elude us. The problem is that often these beliefs have been instilled in us since childhood, and they can be hard to spot because they're so ingrained in our subconscious.

One technique that can be extremely useful is to turn the problem on its head and work from the obvious to the hidden. So, if we're unhappy with any part of our life, we might ask ourselves: 'What underlying belief must I hold to be creating this?' Once we've unearthed it, then we can start to change it.

20

Some people *might* be able to make these changes alone and immediately, because they see the change they want to make as a *decision* rather than a *process*. For example the over-arching decision to no longer be a victim, ever, is one of the most liberating and powerful we can take. As described in the opening chapter, I took just such a decision some years ago and have never looked back. Despite having still managed to create plenty of opportunities for myself to revert to type since then, I hope I can be justifiably proud of the fact that I've stayed strong and not broken my word to myself. If this resonates as you read it, be brave and take the decision yourself. You will never, ever regret it.

But of course it would be naïve and unfair to suggest that all limiting beliefs can be so easily cured as a one-off decision. For some people deeply ingrained beliefs will need more time to shift, and in more severe cases various forms of therapy are available – although we should always be wary of any tendency to offload responsibility when we take this route, because ultimately it's *us* who has to want to change, and *us* who has to make it happen.

The other thing to be aware of is that many of

our limiting beliefs are culturally impressed. Although our modern world is actually much safer, it's far more fear-ridden than in the past. We have insurance companies and medical professionals constantly firing every possible bad scenario at us – the risk of serious illness, or of being robbed, or of our home burning down – and, guess what? If we give these things our attention we run a high risk of attracting them into our life. But there *is* an alternative. We can take ourselves out of the mainstream, dare to be different and simply make the decision, 'I *will not* give these things my attention.'

In fact nowadays it's pretty widely recognised that a high proportion of illness does originate in the mind, at least in adults. That is not to say we're all hypochondriacs, but all mental stresses and strains have to find an outlet in the end, and usually it's in some sort of bodily malady. Eliminating stress and worry from our life as much as possible is an absolute necessity if we want to stay healthy long-term.

Of course some people believe *their* life is just way too busy and complicated for this – but remember that stress doesn't arise from being busy but from feeling we're not in control. So we need to take the control back, in whatever way works for us.

Whatever challenges we're facing, we can make changes to our lifestyle – and even more to our *perception* of our life – that will improve it and give us a degree of control back, if we so *choose*. However desperate we might feel, there is *never* a situation that can't be improved.

Armed with this inspiring knowledge, let's spend some time peering behind the veil to find out how this experience we humans call reality actually works.

to understand the
reality you live in...
learn to understand
the realities you'll
experience after you die

SH*T DOESN'T JUST HAPPEN!!

To help us to peer behind the veil we're extremely fortunate to have access to the hugely important research of a significant number of modern consciousness explorers, who've learned to deliberately take themselves 'out of body', or OOB. We might note that this common description isn't really accurate, because often they're not actually 'travelling' anywhere external to themselves – rather they access other planes of consciousness by 'going within'. In any case the plethora of convincing evidence their brave and pioneering work has placed before us finally provides us with some proper context with which to make sense of the reality we live in.[1]

What they've been describing for some decades, many in books that are still readily available, is that we can access what we think of as the afterlife realms right now – while we're still alive – and explore them as much as we like.

What they've also been telling us is that this

[1] This detailed OOB evidence is presented throughout *Afterlife*, although for a summary of the prime sources see the Appendix.

reality we're experiencing is not as 'real' as we think it is. Or, looking at it another way, there are a great many realities that are all different, but just as real to the consciousnesses experiencing them as ours is to us. What is more they're usually less 'physical' – although again we need to qualify this statement, because to their mostly unenlightened inhabitants many seem just as physical as our reality appears to us. So perhaps we'll call them 'less energetically dense' realms, or realms of 'higher vibration', instead.

Most important for our current purposes, these OOB explorers have all come to realise pretty swiftly that, in these other realms, their expectations, thoughts and emotions control everything that happens. To understand this better, let's look at some examples of what they've discovered about behaviour therein.

They have found that some people die so suddenly they don't even know they're dead, and literally carry on as before in the same earthly surroundings – although somewhat confused to find that other people don't see or talk to them, and that the rules have changed because they can walk through walls and so on.

They have also discovered that others who die suddenly *do* realise what's happened but still cling to the earth experience anyway. Some do this because they simply can't imagine there's anywhere else to go. But others are dominated, for example, by the impulse to take revenge on their murderer, or on a cheating partner; or to complete unfinished projects they think are important; or to try to communicate, usually in vain, with their loved ones – although we might also note that those left behind often exert such a strong energetic pull on the departed, with their intense emotions of loss, that they prevent them from properly moving on.

Others still attach themselves to people who're still alive because they crave the experience of alcohol or drugs, or whatever they themselves were addicted to. Or they can be attracted to someone whose predominant emotion – say anger or lust – matches how they were themselves. In these cases they're trying to get their 'fix' second-hand. But we should be clear that *most* of these 'spirit attachments', while unfortunately troubled, are relatively harmless to their human target.

Slightly more disturbing is the fact that there do

appear to be certain seriously dense realms where the energies of the ex-human inhabitants are so dark, confused and aggressive that they're extremely unpleasant to even pass through. So OOB explorers tend to establish ways of avoiding such realms, and we too would do well to prepare ourselves by making sure our own emotions aren't too heavy and confused after death – otherwise we could be automatically drawn into them.

All this means that the ideas we've developed about ghosts and so on aren't so very far off. It's just that most of us fail to realise that this is a widespread experience, affecting a great many departed souls who have become so immersed in the illusion of life on earth they can't leave.

In fact OOB explorers have repeatedly reported that, with an ever-expanding human population, there's now a huge build-up of souls trapped in what we might call the 'near-earth' and 'lower astral' planes. What is more many of these explorers spend a great deal of time working with entities from the higher realms trying to help those who're trapped to move on. Nevertheless free will always prevails, so those who're insistent on staying stuck will do exactly that. They may even be so wrapped up in their own personal hell of recrimination and self-loathing, perhaps of replaying earthly events over and over again, that they don't even notice there's anyone trying to help them.

In just the same way human explorers pretty quickly realise just how much their thoughts and so on control their experience when their consciousness is no longer restricted to their physical body. Often in their early forays they only have to think briefly about the body they appear to have left behind and zap! they're straight back in it again. Or if they stay in the near-earth plane, although sometimes they report flying above land or sea and enjoying the view, on other occasions they only have to think of a friend or location and zap! they're immediately there.

Even more important for our current purposes, once they start exploring realms of even slightly higher vibration they find their thoughts can influence their entire environment. Moreover that's exactly how it works for people who die and leave our world for good. If they're not bogged down with heavy negative emotions, they're ready for the 'transition' and they believe in some sort of heavenly afterlife, then often they'll experience whatever they conceive that to be.

If it's a crystal castle on a snow-capped mountain, then that's exactly the environment they find themselves in – or a meadow full of wild flowers, a beach with pure white sand, a little shack in the wilderness, an Egyptian temple – the possibilities are endless. But these may be merely temporary and predominantly individual experiences before they move on to something else.

By contrast there are also what modern explorers call 'consensus realities', which are more permanent and can involve significant numbers of souls. Some of the finest examples of these are the religion-based heavens or hells. Yes, these really do exist – and there are as many of them as there have been religions, and different strains of those religions.

If someone is a fervent member of a particular Christian denomination, for example, a host of their predecessors have already created the heavenly version of it purely with their thoughts and expectations. So after death that person may well find themselves going to church and practising exactly the same rituals as before. Many OOB explorers have documented these scenarios in startlingly similar ways.

Effectively each of these realities is just another illusion. So we'd all do well to prepare ourselves for the afterlife by understanding that, while *anything* and *everything* is possible, almost all of it is just another illusion we can move on from. What is more there's no ultimate destination – or at least the afterlife journey never stops, as far as we can tell so far.

The other important thing OOB explorers have learned about these consensus realities is that their own thoughts have far less influence there. This is because the greater the number of souls contributing to a given experience, especially with shared expectations, the harder it is for any one of them or someone from outside to significantly alter it. This fact in particular has a significant bearing on the experience we're having now in the earth plane.

The first thing we need to understand about this reality of ours is that it operates at a relatively low level of vibration – meaning our thoughts and expectations don't influence it with anything like the rapidity of some of the higher vibratory planes. Instead there's a significant time delay. Indeed space-time itself is much more prevalent in our reality than in many others. This is why, when we're immersed in it, we can't travel at the 'speed of thought' as in higher realms – unless we significantly alter our state of consciousness.

Ours is also very much a consensus reality. This adds to the delays in seeing our thoughts feed through into our experience, because they have to be processed alongside all the myriad, often conflicting, thoughts of the other people who have an influence on that bit of our shared reality, whatever it is.

Sport provides us with a wonderful example of this. In the opening chapter we discussed the fact that sports psychology is big business in our modern world. So, apart from the physical training, the honing of skills and so on, the greater the mental focus a sportsperson puts into their desired outcome – an Olympic gold medal or whatever – the greater their chance of achieving it. They do this partly by using their *thoughts* and *imagination* – that is by visualising the desired outcome happening – and partly by setting up a hugely intense *expectation* of success, and maintaining that intensity for a long time.

Many people, when confronted with the idea that they're creating the *entirety* of their own reality, respond that this can't be true precisely because we're only *co*-creating it alongside everyone else – so their behaviours and decisions must be having an impact on our experience. This sounds so intuitively correct that it can be a hard idea to shift. Indeed the sporting example seems to prove that we can't always create the outcome we desire, however much we believe in it, precisely because of the competing desires of others.

But the research that led me to write *The Power of You* revealed that the vast majority of what can reasonably be described as the best-known sources of channelled wisdom from the last fifty years – that is Seth, Abraham, Neale Donald Walsch's 'God', Ramtha, Elias, Bashar, Jeshua and the Pathwork Guide – were all in remarkable accord on this issue.[2] Indeed it struck me that the consistency of their view that the law of attraction reigns *supreme* over everything we experience, at least as adults, was something that had perhaps been somewhat overlooked.

In other words they're adamant that, although we are indeed co-creating this experience alongside others, *everything* each of us experiences is *only* a reflection of our *own* thoughts and beliefs. What is more this is true for every single one of us. This is such a crucial issue that I've reproduced a number of key extracts from their messages to illustrate the point:[3]

> Physiological reality, take me literally, is a mirror, it is just a more complex mirror, a holographic mirror, a multidimensional mirror, so that you don't always recognize all the reflections as you. But believe me,

[2] For more information on these sources see the Appendix.
[3] For further details and sources see *The Power of You*, chapter 3.

they are, all the reflections are you, and I mean literally every object, person, place and thing, every situation, every circumstance, every moment of time and space is you being reflected back to yourself. (Bashar)

The power of that energy, as it creates that shockwave that extends outwardly, generates an action as a magnet, the most powerful magnet that you can imagine. That magnet will pull to it any expression that matches what you are projecting. It will intentionally seek out any expression, any manifestation that matches the energy that is being expressed. (Elias)

The first step in awakening is to allow into the mind this axiom of truth: nothing that you experience is caused by anything outside of you. You experience only the effects of your own choices. (Jeshua)

As I have often said, the sum total of all your conscious, semi-conscious, unconscious, explicit and implicit thoughts, beliefs, assumptions, intentions, feelings, emotions and will directions — conflicting as they may be — creates your present experience and the way your life unfolds for you. Your present life expresses your inner state exactly, like a faultless mathematical equation. (The Pathwork Guide)

Your own physical reality is created in perfect replica of your inner desires and thoughts. (Seth)

The universe is just a big Xerox machine. It simply produces multiple copies of your thoughts. (Neale Donald Walsch's 'God')

We can only marvel at the sort of underlying dynamic processes that ensure all of our experiences come together and dovetail in such a way that each one of us is only ever having our *own* thoughts and beliefs reflected back to us in the experiences we share with others, and in the behaviour they exhibit towards us. But that's exactly what these wisest of channelled sources insist is happening.

Because ours is a consensus reality it operates according to a set of rules we've built up over time, based on our experiences. Nowhere is this more in evidence than in the fact that objects and people *appear* physical to us. Actually our brains and accompanying senses and organs have evolved to be hard-wired to perceive them as such.

So we simply don't believe we can pass our hand straight through a table. But we can.

If that's just too big as an initial conceptual step, think of the well-known anecdotes of desperate mothers lifting heavy cars to rescue their trapped child. Are they obeying the normal laws of physics as we commonly understand them when they do that? Of course not. The intensity of their emotion, of their desire and, above all, of their *belief* that they can and must save their child, produces a momentary suspension of those laws.

Such a feat can be achieved by anyone at any time, as long as they have the requisite belief. Indeed in the companion volume *What Jesus Was Really Saying* I contend that Christ was trying to show us through his supposed miracles that each and every one of us, no matter how apparently high or low, is a powerful 'creator god' who can manipulate this illusion we call reality at will, if only we have sufficient belief.

Recognition that the reality we inhabit is actually in large part an illusion should not be mistaken for criticism of our way of life or of the consensus reality we've developed. Our earth plane is an extremely useful environment in which to gather experience – which, as we'll see in the next chapter, is all consciousness ever wants to do.

For now the point to appreciate is that the reality we've chosen to experience is an *extremely* persuasive illusion. Yet being able to see it as such, even if only to a relatively limited extent, can significantly enhance our experience of it – and make it a lot less painful too.

As humans, many of us are addicted to suffering. But we don't *have* to suffer. In truth we *all* have the capability to shape our human experience into *whatever* we want it to be, subject to a few constraints that we'll discuss later. Yet even if we don't create the perfect life for ourselves – whatever that might be – and only manage to influence our experience to a more limited extent, that's still a huge improvement over feeling we're constantly being buffeted by outrageous fortune; or that we're at the mercy of our karma, or of a God who's at best unpredictable and at worst downright spiteful.

It is perfectly reasonable to have doubts about all this, especially on first exposure to what can seem extremely radical ideas. But it might help to remember that even modern scientists are having to massively broaden their view of what constitutes reality – and are increasingly having to enter the realms of *meta*physics to do it.

Their work at the quantum level indicates that dimensionality is probably much more complex than the three of space and one of time we're used to perceiving. Also that what appears to be physical matter is, at least in one sense, not physical at all – it's just energy fields vibrating at different rates. In simpler terms they'll tell you that the vast majority of any atom is just empty space. Harder still to imagine is the idea that time itself is something of an illusion, as we'll discover later.

Even more interesting are modern studies into what consciousness really is, and where it comes from. Suffice to say we should be in no doubt that it's far more intelligent and logical to form our view of the world based on the multitude of modern evidence that our experience isn't just a 'physical' one, than it is to adopt the materialist view that the brain is the source of consciousness and that everything ends at death.[4]

So let's be clear. We are fundamentally *spiritual* beings having a *human* experience, rather than the other way around.

Which still begs the million-dollar question: *why are we here at all?*

[4] For details of the evidence for the non-materialist view see *Afterlife*, Part 1.

your true soul consciousness is interested in one thing, and one thing alone... to expand itself through different experiences

SH*T DOESN'T JUST HAPPEN!!

To properly examine this question we must begin by injecting a little complexity, although it'll be kept to a minimum. For many decades now some scientists and cosmologists have been talking about the 'many worlds' interpretation of quantum theory, or the idea that multiple parallel universes exist alongside each other. At its most extreme this means that every single choice or interaction that has ever been made has created a new universe, so that there are already an almost infinite number that are only minutely differentiated. But arguably this a somewhat philosophically inelegant worldview.

Nevertheless modern OOB explorers have found that there are indeed multiple universes or realities. Some of these seem to be very much like earth except with certain marked differences – such as having gone down a different route with respect to relatively primitive technology for lighting, heating and motive power, for example. But they've also encountered various consensus realities with widely varying types of existence – some of them not so human and earth-like, and some involving less intense emotions than ours, or less apparent physicality. It appears the possibilities in this respect are literally endless, and arguably this far broader worldview makes much more sense.

The first conclusion we can draw from this is that it's one thing for materialist science to be concentrating on locating life forms in other parts of our known universe – of which there may indeed be vast numbers on other planets that support 'physical' life. But it's quite another to understand that even this search is only scratching the surface by concentrating on just one universe that operates at a particular level of vibration. It seems that even our broadest possible concept of *our* universe and *our* reality is just the tiniest speck in the totality of all the realities that exist at different levels of vibration and frequency.

So what is creating these different realities, and why? We have already seen that the consciousnesses of human beings who've left the earth plane for good create their own environments and realities with their thoughts, expectations and so on. But who or what creates the broader conditions and opportunities for these to come into being in the first place? Is it some sort of God?

In recent decades many people have turned away from the idea of an independent, omnipotent *being*, characterised in Christian iconography as an old man with a grey beard sitting on a fluffy cloud. They resonate more with the Eastern concept of an ultimate 'Source' or universal consciousness that's inherent *within* all of creation rather than external to it.

The related concept of an ultimate, universal, undifferentiated, perfected One-ness, perhaps consisting only of pure, unconditional love, is highly attractive to many of us. What is more many spiritual searchers claim to have made contact with this One-ness in meditation or by other means of inducing expanded states, and such transcendental experiences usually have a profound impact. Nevertheless even these may not be what they seem, as we'll see in the next chapter.

Moreover there are alternatives to this view. One of the most intriguing and arguably persuasive scientific theories I've come across suggests that the existence of an almost infinitely varied collection of universes and realities can be explained using only two propositions.[5] Although on first exposure it's an uncomfortable idea for most people, the first is that the primal cause underlying everything was not some sort of perfected Source energy, but an entirely primitive and undifferentiated consciousness. The second is that all consciousness ever wants to do is to 'lower its entropy' – or, in simple terms, to organise itself better. This idea at least partly mirrors those esoteric teachings that refer to the primal source 'creating order out of chaos'.

How does consciousness do this? By diversifying into differentiated units, each one capable of creating new and ever more sophisticated realities, and each one in turn projecting individualised aspects of itself into those realities. The purpose being? To *experience*. Nothing more, nothing less. So consciousness lowers its entropy by experiencing – or, as an alternative way of looking at it, *expanding*.

---

[5] For a summary of nuclear physicist and long-time OOB explorer Thomas Campbell's 'Big Theory of Everything' see *Supersoul*, chapter 5.

Theories like this are based on the idea that, underneath the many illusions, all levels of reality are essentially information-based and digital. So it can be useful to think of these various realities as endless computer-style simulation games being played out by different levels of consciousness. As long, that is, as this doesn't conjure up images of humanity being slaves to whoever's in control of the game, because that's absolutely *not* what's being described here. Instead every level of consciousness in these various simulations is operating with complete free will.

There is a whole world of difference between the controlling nature of organised religion and the liberation and empowerment of true spirituality. The latter is much less interested in developing moral frameworks and codes of behaviour. So do *any* moral judgments remain relevant when we're postulating an essentially digital reality?

We saw in the last chapter that, although OOB explorers have encountered hellish-type realms, like any others these have only been created by the thoughts and expectations of departed souls

– who in this case are tormenting and punishing *themselves* to varying degrees.

So, despite the mythology of St Peter sitting at the gates of heaven, or of Osiris 'weighing the heart' in the Egyptian underworld, it's clear there's no judgment from on high or eternal damnation awaiting those who apparently do wrong. Nor is there a devil who tempts weak people into his domain or dreams up ever more shocking punishments for human miscreants.

In fact there's a general consensus among secular scholars that such concepts were introduced by an early Christian Church who understood all too well that people who're scared can be controlled. Nor were they alone, because some Hindu texts make the Christian hell sound like a holiday. What is more it's a technique still used very successfully by many of our governments today. At the heart of all this is usually a desire to hold onto, indeed amass, ever more power over others – and, of course, money.

All this in turn means there's no such thing as *evil* either, and that any moral codes we develop are purely subjective. This is a really difficult concept for many people to take on board – indeed to some it's downright offensive – so it needs some explaining.

Of course any group of people large or small has to agree a certain set of rules that allow everyone to live together in some sort of harmony. But is there any real objectivity in all this? After all, each of our main religions has its own moral code and, although there are certain general similarities, in many respects they're substantially different. They can't all be right, can they?

In the same way most modern societies regard murder as a major crime that carries a heavy punishment, but it wasn't always that way – in the American 'Wild West', for example. Even the age at which it's considered appropriate to have sex and marry has altered massively from one culture to another.

The truth is there's no *objective* right or wrong, there's *only* the moral judgments we humans choose to adopt in any given time, place and cultural setting. So we'd do well to recognise that any rules a society collectively decides to live by are nothing more than a convenience.

They have no objectivity, there's no definitive moral code, and there's certainly no such thing as inherent or pure evil.

We will return to the issue of apparently evil acts or people shortly. But, generally speaking, can we really be so apparently blasé about a human experience that sometimes involves so much suffering?

The answer is that we sometimes need to take a step back so we can attempt to adopt more of a soul perspective on the matter – indeed attempt to work out how that more divine part of us, or what we might for now call our 'true soul consciousness', might look at it. Recalling the analogy of a computer game, it knows that our human experience can best be compared to that of an actor in a play, where what happens to the character doesn't affect the actor themselves – at least not permanently.

The problem is that once we're playing our human role we tend to get so incredibly caught up in it that we forget who we really are, and allow it to cause us all sorts of pain and suffering. But we can *choose* to see it for what it is, and even to *change* the play or the scene if we don't like it.

What is more, once we understand that our true soul consciousness is interested only in expanding itself through different experiences, we can come to see that *everything* that happens in our world is a valid addition to the universal databank of experience. However much we may judge others or even ourselves as humans, no judgment is attached to *anything* at the soul level – not least because, at the end of the day, no *permanent* damage is done to the actors in the play, be they apparently victim or perpetrator. Our underlying energy or consciousness can never be destroyed, or even harmed – even if many of us do allow ourselves to fall under the illusion of suffering, not just in this world but sometimes in the next too.

Nevertheless one other major motivation does exist, in our reality at least, as a fundamental rule. Ours is often described as a 'dualistic' environment because it involves contrasts or apparent polarities. We can now see that it's clearly inappropriate to think of these as merely 'good versus evil', or even 'good versus bad'. Some people try to take the element of judgment out and talk more in terms of 'positive versus negative', but even that doesn't really get to the heart of the duality.

What *does* is the understanding that, as human beings, we have a primary level of choice. Every single time we react to a circumstance or person, or make a decision, we choose the path of *love* or that of *fear*. In some of the higher realms duality doesn't exist at all, so love is a given, but in ours taking the loving option is always a *choice*.

Practical examples of fear-based reactions and emotions include worry, pessimism, fear of losing possessions or love, judgment of others, impatience, greed, guilt and unkindness – and, at their worst, hatred, bitterness, revenge and so on. The love-based ones, on the other hand, include optimism, calmness, patience, forgiveness, empathy, kindness, selflessness, generosity and humour.

So how does this fit with the primary universal motivation of consciousness always wanting to expand itself via experience, irrespective of what that experience is? The answer is that, in our dualistic reality, any loving response will tend to produce far more of an expansion of consciousness than a fear-based one – and, except in a very few extreme cases, will literally make us *feel* far better. For the vast majority of people this is an inherent part of our human programming.

Admittedly some individuals are born into circumstances so far removed from love that they struggle to experience or project it ever, in any form at all – and these are the ones some people would call *evil*. But we should recognise by now that this is just another judgment.

How do we know how we'd react if we'd been born into their environment, and been through what they went through? Of course we've all seen shining examples of people born in difficult circumstances who've gone on to lead exemplary lives – and we've also seen the opposite, where rich, spoilt children go astray. But without exactly experiencing someone else's life we simply can't make any judgment. We *can* proudly proclaim: '*I* would *never* allow myself to behave like that!' – and we can *hope* that's true. But, because we've never actually faced the totality of that person's experience, we just can't be so sure.

SH*T DOESN'T JUST HAPPEN!!

This in turn leads us onto the question that has baffled and perplexed ever since we invented the idea of a single, supreme deity: how can one individual be born with all the advantages of a family where there's plenty of money and love to go round, while another suffers abject poverty and all the worst excesses of degradation and lack – of love, money, everything?

At some point most of us allow ourselves to wonder what kind of supreme being allows that degree of inequality and apparent unfairness, just as we ask how wonderful people who don't seem to deserve it can die young – even as children who had their whole lives ahead of them. When the only answer monotheistic religions can offer is that 'God moves in mysterious ways', it can be enough to drive us away completely.

It was for me, as a teenager. I proudly proclaimed myself an atheist for two decades until I was introduced to the traditional idea of reincarnation. The argument ran that if we each have many lives we get to experience all the different extremes, and everything ends up fair for all. For many years I found this view persuasive, simple and elegant. Indeed I wrote about it at length in my *Books of the Soul* series.

But, as we saw in the opening chapter, my recent research has taken me down a rather different path.

there's no external **God**, only
the divinity of who you really
are... a projection of a
supersoul consciousness so
creatively powerful that you're
a god in your own right

SH*T DOESN'T JUST HAPPEN!!

The thing that really started me down this new route was a series of meetings in the Autumn of 2012 with a good friend who is also an experienced OOB explorer.[6] He explained that on several recent excursions he'd encountered an entity far wiser and more powerful than any he'd previously met – indeed so wise and powerful that initially he couldn't cope with its energy field for more than a short time.

Does this sound familiar? It is somewhat reminiscent of other near-death and OOB experiences reported down the ages in which people encounter what they take to be God, Jesus or some other prophet whose energy can sometimes be overwhelming. So was my friend actually meeting God?

As it turns out, no. As he became more used to this entity, and as the entity itself toned down its energy to make it easier for him to be in its presence, he came to realise that it was actually another aspect of *his own self*. Moreover this was not in a 'we're all one' way, because to him

[6] Details of my discussions with Todd Acamesis can be found in *Supersoul*, chapter 1.

it was clearly an individualised consciousness and not some sort of universal Source. Nevertheless its power and wisdom left him in no doubt that in our terms it was supremely 'divine'.

So I started reading all the OOB literature I could find, and sure enough other pioneers had had similar experiences with individualised divine beings they knew to be other aspects of themselves. Moreover various sources of channelled material seemed to be describing something similar.[7]

It wasn't long before I sensed that I needed a new word to describe these divine beings. Some of the pioneers referred to them as their *higher selves*, and under traditional reincarnation models this does tend to mean the 'core' soul energy we supposedly reconnect with at some point after death – allowing us a broader perspective across our past lives and so on. But under traditional models this higher self is still clearly a work in progress that's 'growing' from

[7] For details of both sets of evidence see *Supersoul*, chapters 3 and 4.

one life to the next, and that's not what the OOB explorers were describing at all. Some of them favoured the word *oversoul* instead, but this too can be confusing because it's often used to refer to God or Source itself.

What is more, I came to realise that the OOB evidence was all tending to suggest that we carry on identifying with the personality of the life we've just left after death, continuing to have all sorts of experiences in both individual and consensus realities in other planes.[8] Contrary to traditional reincarnation models I could find no evidence in this plethora of material for a guaranteed merger with any sort of higher self or core soul energy – or at least not one that happened any time soon after death. Nor did I find widespread references to souls getting ready to reincarnate on earth – in fact there was really only one, and that not entirely convincing.

This view was reinforced by a variety of material channelled from ordinary individuals who'd

---

[8] For evidence of the survival of the life personality see *Supersoul*, chapter 6.

passed over, as opposed to that obtained from wise entities such as Seth or Abraham as mentioned in an earlier chapter. Some of this was to be found in fascinating and often-overlooked books from earlier in the last century.[9]

For these reasons I felt I needed to preserve the word *soul* to describe the relatively low-level consciousness or awareness that many of us seem to retain for some time after leaving the earth plane. So the new word I chose for our true, divine or higher soul consciousness was, of course, the *super*soul.

How then does our supersoul relate to any concept of God or Source? The evidence would suggest that as a human being the former is as close as we'll ever get to understanding what true divinity is, and it's why we can reasonably make the claim that each of us is a god in our own right. Using the concept of simulated game-style realities discussed in the last chapter,

[9] The details of this OOB and channelled material about the ongoing experiences of the life personality after death are presented throughout *Afterlife*.

supersouls would appear to be the very entities who create whole new universes, which operate under totally different rules, whenever they feel like changing and expanding the game. But each supersoul is still very much an individual entity and, to provide some context, it seems likely that myriads of supersouls are involved just in this game we call 'life on planet earth'.

Our supersoul, then, is far, far removed from any concept of a universal Source consciousness. But it also seems possible that anyone who thinks they've made even fleeting contact with this consciousness – or whatever they want to call that incredible sense of oneness, stillness and peace that some are fortunate enough to experience via deep meditation or other expanded states – may be mistaken. Rather it may well be that that's what contact just with our *own supersoul* feels like.

So this is the definition of the supersoul I came up with:

A supersoul is a grouping of hundreds, maybe thousands, of souls. Myriads of supersouls are projecting individual soul aspects of themselves into this and myriad other realities, meaning they are very far from the ultimate consciousness. Yet to be fully connected to your supersoul is to have boundless wisdom and creative power, and as a full holographic representation of it you are already more divine than you can hope to conceive – divine enough, even, to nullify further speculation about what lies beyond.

The other piece of evidence that supports the concept of the supersoul came to me some time later and was what drew me to write *The Power of You*. As discussed in an earlier chapter it's the consistent message from the wisest channelled sources that the law of attraction reigns supreme over how we ourselves create the reality we each experience.

More than this, though, the further message from these various sources is that, even as apparently limited human beings, our creative power is actually boundless if we did but know it. Indeed they go further still and insist that it's finally time for us to recognise that we *ourselves* are the creator gods we have so long sought.

Talking of *time*, this too is a concept that needs

to be reappraised if we're to gain a proper understanding of the underlying workings of our reality.

everything is happening
in 'the now'...
however much we're conditioned
to experience time

SH*T DOESN'T JUST HAPPEN!!

We are becoming increasingly familiar with the idea that we must stay in the moment, or 'in the now' as it's often called. Although this advice has been embodied in all the wisest spiritual literature throughout the ages, it's been given wonderful poignancy for our complex and demanding modern world by authors such as Eckhart Tolle in his *Power of Now*.

This is one of the mantras used by sports psychologists. For example their advice to a golfer or tennis player would be: 'Forget about the bad shot you played just now. Don't let your mind wander to what the consequences would be if you were to lose the match. Just concentrate on what you can control, which is the shot you're playing right now.'

In the same way Tolle says we should leave the past behind because it's already happened and we can't change it, while we should never worry about the future because it hasn't happened yet – especially if we're prone to assuming the worst, which can only make that outcome more likely. He suggests that we should only concern ourselves with the future if there's some action we can take *now* to head off a problem or to make a desired outcome more likely.

SH*T DOESN'T JUST HAPPEN!!

One corollary is, of course, that if we spend all our time worrying about the past or future then we're liable to miss the potential beauty of what's happening right now, right in front of us. The wonderful scenery, or the kindness of a friend listening while we catalogue our woes, and so on. The ancient Chinese philosopher Lao Tzu sums all this up beautifully: 'If you are depressed you are living in the past. If you are anxious you are living in the future. If you are at peace you are living in the present.' This also means that the more we live in the present the more likely it is that we'll be approaching life from a place of love rather than one of fear.

An even more important corollary is the fact that it's what we're thinking and believing right now that will create what we experience in the future. The wonderful channelled source Seth, who we quoted in an earlier chapter, embodies this wisdom in the key phrase 'the present is your point of power'.

But, more than this, is there really any such thing as the past or the future?

There are a few basic facts about time that we

should establish before we can properly appreciate how it works. We all know from personal experience that it can seem to play strange tricks. For example, when we're completely immersed in something we love and are giving it our full attention, time speeds up – that is, hours can pass in what seems like a matter of minutes. By contrast when we're waiting for something outside of our control and have nothing else to engage our attention, time can drag and minutes can feel like hours. So our experience of elapsed time is very much a matter of perception.

From a scientific perspective Einstein's general theory of relativity established that time and space are interwoven and always relative to the observer. For example, when astronomers are observing the universe through a powerful telescope they're actually seeing a broad range of the 'past' because of the amount of time it takes for the light from distant stars to travel to earth. Similarly because of the incredible density of a black hole, time slows down in the vicinity until the 'event horizon' is reached, inside which it has slowed so much that even light can't escape.

SH*T DOESN'T JUST HAPPEN!!

From all this we can see that in no sense is time a fixed constant, especially across massive distances or when huge velocities are involved. This notwithstanding the fact that we've built incredibly accurate devices to measure its passing in the local environment of our planet.

Further revelations about time come from the OOB pioneers. We saw in an earlier chapter that in many other realities thought instantaneously translates into experience. It is only in denser realities like ours that space-time produces a lag between the two.

Discussions such as these are hugely taxing to our human brains, especially because we're deliberately designed to experience time as a continuum or flow of events *from* the past, *through* the present and *into* the future. This is what allows us to operate in this reality at all, for a variety of reasons.

First, without being able to filter out most of our experiences and file them away in the drawer marked 'past', our brains would quickly overload. Second, to gain experience in this realm – and, remember, that's our only objective – it's really useful to rely on the concept of cause and effect. Indeed without it our species would never have survived. We need the understanding that *if* I put my hand in the fire *then* it hurts, and *if* I don't remove it *then* my hand will be destroyed.

But, as the wisest gurus and philosophers down the ages have all tried to explain, the experience of time as a continuum is merely our human *perception*. So what's the secret to understanding what time really is, and how it really works?

A number of our channelled sources talk about time as a *series of snapshots* rather than as a continuous flow, and also about the concept of *vertical* rather than *horizontal* time. Building on this I've attempted to put together the following definition:

> *Time is a series of discrete snapshots of an eternal now that encompasses everything that we perceive as the past and future, but is nevertheless forever changing from now-moment to now-moment.*

Again I'm very much aware that this is intended to be a simple book, and that once more we're straying into complex territory. But it's worth trying to visualise this revised conception of time if we're to have any proper understanding of how our reality actually works underneath our limited perceptions.

Imagine an abacus placed on its side, with a series of vertical wires with multiple beads on each one. The central 'row' of beads represents the present, while the rows above and below it represent the future and the past respectively. Each column is a snapshot of a given now-moment, which encapsulates not only the total state of our reality in that moment's present (represented by the central bead) but *also* the totality of all past now-moments (represented by the beads below it) *and* the totality of all future now-moments, i.e. the most likely projected simulations of the game based on past experience and decisions and so on (represented by the beads above it).

As we move to the right from one now-moment to the next, each bead drops down one row and moves right into the next column. So what was the most likely state of our reality in the next now-moment becomes crystallised into whatever reality we've actually created for ourselves in the new now-moment – which may or may not be similar depending on how many decisions were substantially different from what was expected. Meanwhile the now-moment just passed drops below the central line and into the actualised past of the new now-moment.

This is very hard to visualise without a diagram and some proper mathematical identification of the various beads or now-moments.[10] But even if the above has only provided a vague sense of how our perception of time as a continuous flow doesn't reflect what's really going on, hopefully our minds are still freed up to accept fewer limitations.

For our current purposes there's one hugely important implication of the fact that everything is happening in the now, and that time as we perceive it doesn't really exist, especially in the higher realms. It is that the various soul aspects or life personalities projected by the supersoul are in reality all operating *alongside* each other

[10] For a more comprehensive diagrammatic explanation see *Supersoul*, chapter 6.

in the eternal now, irrespective of what human era appears to be involved.

So that aspect of our supersoul who's acting out the part of a medieval knight, of an Egyptian princess, of a caveman or whatever is still alive and kicking. Even though it's so hard for us to imagine, their life is still ongoing. This means there can be no *past* lives because they're all happening *at the same time*.

Corroboration of this crucial fact is supplied by various of our wisest channelled sources.[11] Here are several excellent examples of their views:

> What you understand of reincarnation, and of the time terms involved, is a very simplified tale indeed... Reincarnation, in its own way, is also a parable. It seems very difficult for you to understand that you live in many realities – and many centuries – at one time. (Seth)

> You are also living other lives – what you call 'past lives' – right now as well, although you experience them as having

[11] For details see *The Power of You*, chapter 2.

71

been in your 'past'. (Neale Donald Walsch's 'God')

Anyone who reads the entirety of the powerful channelled evidence I've collated will surely come to appreciate that the whole ensemble of lives in which we and our fellow soul projections are engaged is an ongoing, dynamic and interactive process.

This in turn has some hugely important implications, as we're just about to find out.

there's no 'past' karma unless
you choose to believe in it...
and patterns only repeat if
you choose to let them

SH*T DOESN'T JUST HAPPEN!!

In modern spiritual literature lip service has regularly been paid to the idea that all lives are happening at the same time. But most people soon revert back to the simple comforts of the traditional reincarnation model, because trying to understand the concept of simultaneous lives is just too hard. But perhaps now we have to be brave if we're going to take the next big step.

Admittedly the way in which I wrestled with various matrix-style models of soul consciousness when producing the first two editions of *Supersoul* can make for challenging reading. But the 'synthesised matrix model' I ended up with has a number of practical implications that actually provide a much simpler understanding of how life might really work compared to more traditional models.[12]

Perhaps the most obvious is that it logically implies there can be no such thing as karma being carried *from* one life *to* the next. The underlying dynamics of our lives simply can't

[12] For background evidence and diagrammatic explanations of the various models I worked through to arrive at this, see *Supersoul*, chapters 6 and 7.

work in such a simplistic way if all lives are simultaneous.

When confronted with this new model many people try to argue that our lives must be *both* simultaneous *and* consecutive – and I accept that the 'both... and' principle does often underlie spiritual philosophy. It is fundamental, for example, to the concept of the 'holographic soul' that I developed some years ago, which in amended form suggests that we're *both* individual projections of our supersoul, *and* full holographic representations of it, all at the same time.[13]

However I've spent several years with the new model now and I'm entirely unable to see how this principle can apply here. This is because we need to establish what the implications of any model of soul consciousness are, and in this case I'm convinced we can't have it both ways – inasmuch as the implications of any simultaneous-life model are so hugely different

---

[13] For a full definition and explanation see *Supersoul*, chapters 2 and 8, and also www.ianlawton.com/holsoul.html.

from, and incompatible with, those of a consecutive-life one.

If our new model is correct the next question we must logically ask is, who or what are the souls that people make contact with during, for example, past-life regression? If I'm to be completely candid, having spent some years training as a regression therapist – which also involves undergoing many sessions acting as the client – I'm well aware that it's hardly impossible for the human psyche to fabricate details of apparent past lives so that current-life trauma can be more easily processed. This is because of their greater degree of separation.

From a therapeutic point of view most practitioners accept that it makes very little difference whether any past lives recalled are genuine or not. But it would be entirely disingenuous of me to now suggest that all apparently past-life memories are false. I spent many years collating and analysing what I considered to be the best cases of veridical past-life recall – that is, those involving incredibly obscure details that were subsequently verified – and they cannot just be jettisoned because they might no longer fit neatly with our new model.[14]

The conclusion I've come to is that if the lives encountered at least under *therapeutic* conditions have any validity, then they're most likely to be those of what I've chosen to call 'resonant souls'. Under our new model these would be sibling projections from our supersoul with whom we have an especially close connection – for example because of strongly shared traits or challenges, or because their experiences act as a significant contrast to our own. Inasmuch as they're projections of the same supersoul they can still be seen as other aspects of ourselves. But we need to be clear that in another sense they and we are very much independent entities.

This is important because various of our wise channelled sources suggest that we genuinely interact with these resonant souls, precisely because their life experiences are still ongoing, whatever apparent human era they're operating

[14] For details of what I consider to be the best-known cases, categorised as either weak, inconclusive or unexplained, see *The Big Book of the Soul*, chapter 3.

in. They add that these interactions *tend* to occur at a subconscious or subliminal level.[15]

So, even if karma isn't being carried over from one life to another, the key question is now this. Can these resonant souls operating alongside us have a *significant* influence on our lives – sufficient to interfere with our ability to create whatever reality we choose for ourselves?

Of course the logical answer is that, in order for the law of attraction to reign supreme, each actor in each play must be responsible for their *own* experience – and for the entirety of what they create in that experience as they go along via their *own* thoughts, intentions, beliefs and so on. It would completely violate our free will if some other actor in some other apparent timeframe was having a major impact on us, perhaps without us even being aware of it.

The good news, at least for those who like to take full responsibility, is that this view is emphatically endorsed by our wisest channelled

[15] For full details of these interactions and their implications see *Supersoul*, chapter 7.

sources.[16] Here again are selected examples:

> Your lives exist simultaneously. They are other expressions of yourself, interacting, but with each conscious self possessing the point of power in its own present. (Seth)

> All of your focuses are continuously influencing of each other and of this focus, as you also are continuously influencing of all of your other focuses. But your attention is in *this* focus, and your creations in this focus are *your* creations. They are purposeful, they are intentional, and they are the responsibility of this particular focus. Therefore, as you continue to direct your attention to this particular focus in which you hold your attention, you also empower yourselves much more and create much more of your own expression of freedom and your ability to manipulate energy intentionally within this focus... You *do* create your reality individually...

---

[16] For details see *The Power of You*, chapter 2.

> Your choices *are* your choices. You hold
> free will. You are not subject or victim to
> *any* expression of energy within *any* area
> of consciousness. (Elias)

They could hardly make the position much
clearer for us.

Let us take a moment to consider an example
from my own life. In the opening chapter I
mentioned the victim mentality that I allowed to
build up some years back. Although I was
operating from a traditional reincarnation model
at the time, when I finally recognised it for what
it was I didn't try to work out what supposed
past lives might have caused my experience and
try to heal them at source. I just made a
conscious decision in the now that victimhood
was no longer going to be part of who I am.

That decision was fully tested only shortly
afterwards when the partner with whom I'd
been having a long-distance relationship for
several years finally ended it by meeting
someone else and falling even more in love with
him than she'd been with me. It was hugely
painful, but I didn't allow myself to fall back into

old habits, despite sore temptation.

Yet it was only as I was writing *The Gift* shortly afterwards that I remembered one of the very first apparently past lives I'd experienced when I was training as a regression therapist some years before. This involved a boy whose brother married the love of both of their lives. It appeared that he let his sense of victimhood and rejection take over to such an extent that he spent forty years living alone, staring out at the nearby fields, before he finally died. My traditional take on this at the time was that when I was similarly rejected in favour of someone else in this life I conquered a challenge that had completely overwhelmed me in that other life – this time choosing to react with love rather than bitterness and self-pity.

But using our new model I'd now suggest that, if that other personality has any validity at all, he's not *me* per se – instead he's most likely a resonant soul from my supersoul facing a similar challenge to the one I faced. I hope that what I achieved at the time may have helped him, given that in a sense that even I find hard to fully understand his life must be simultaneous and therefore still ongoing, and I'm sure it will if he's open to that guidance. But – and this is the key point – there was no need at all for me to have any awareness of him to take the conscious decisions I did about how I responded to the challenge of rejection in my own life.

More interesting still, I was given the 'gift' of handling the situation by smothering it with love by a gentle but authoritative voice inside my own head, which kicked in the first time the potential heartache of imagining the two of them together arose. I am not particularly sensitive to such voices, but this one spoke to me loud and clear. Who was this talking to me? I cannot be certain. But just maybe it was another aspect of my supersoul who had themselves mastered this challenge, and was passing on some hugely wise and timely advice – that I was fortunately open enough to listen to.

To finish this section, of course if anyone *chooses* to believe they have karma carried over from one or more apparent past lives, that is simply one of the attitudes that will influence the experience they create for themselves, to a greater or lesser extent. But, without wishing to be disrespectful about beliefs held by a great many people, *if* our new model is correct then they have no real foundation. Of course, if such beliefs help a person to better cope with trauma, one can rightly ask 'what's the harm?' But if they result in a tendency to avoid responsibility for the experiences being created in this life, and particularly in any sense of predestination or even victimhood, then arguably they're unhelpful and limiting.

The alternative under our new model is to choose to believe our sources when they say that no other resonant soul can have any significant impact on our experience. The only possible proviso is that we might choose to let them in certain circumstances, if we believe this to be beneficial.

If we turn now from apparently past lives to our current life, our entire human conditioning is to use associations from what we perceive as past events to determine how we'll act in any given now-moment. It was fundamental to our survival as a species in the early years, and still is now to some extent. When we were discussing cause and effect in the last chapter we considered how we all learn early on that if we put our hand into a flame it hurts, and so on, and this also forms a past association – and a very useful one at that.

The trouble is we carry this over into all areas of our life, and can often use past associations in an unhealthy way – for example, to bolster a sense of victimhood. How often do we hear people say, 'I always attract the wrong sort of partner', or 'if there's bad luck going it will find me', or 'I'm always broke and never have enough money'?

Even those who mainly adopt a positive outlook on life will probably have one or two areas where their past association is with apparent failure. So, recalling the observer self from an earlier chapter, we should always be on the lookout for any limiting statements like this we might make.

As for those who tend to be primarily stuck in cycles of negativity, the key is to somehow break the chain and recognise that life doesn't *have* to be like that. Each new situation that comes along doesn't *have* to follow the same script as before. We *can* change it, simply by refusing to let past associations play a part.

Once we get the ball rolling, again it'll fall to our observer self to notice when we're lapsing into old patterns and to change the tape.

For example, instead of saying to ourselves, 'my new job is wonderful but my bosses will probably end up exploiting me just like all the others', we can insist that they're *not* any of the bosses we've worked with before, and there's no reason for them to behave in the same way – because this is a fresh start. But of course this must be accompanied by a genuine belief that we *deserve* proper respect in the workplace, which must over-ride any old subconscious beliefs involving lack of self worth and so on. Otherwise we'll just attract another set of bosses who'll be only too happy to demonstrate that these beliefs still exist within us.

It is the same if we've had a string of relationships that have gone badly, or if we continually find ourselves lonely or short of money, or with any other situation where we want to break the chain and change the programme.

In fact again, rather than letting it be a process, we can make a *decision* to break all ties with any particular pattern of previous experience. Remember from the last chapter the suggestion that the future of the game is simulated based on the most likely decisions each of us will make, based in turn on previous choices? Well, we can *choose* to make entirely different decisions that can massively alter the course of that simulated future.

In truth, because time isn't a continuum, as true masters we could theoretically *choose* to recreate ourselves *completely afresh* in each new now-moment. The sky is pretty much the limit, subject to a few restrictions that we'll consider in the next chapter.

But for most of us it will be sufficient to know that, particularly if we're not happy with the current state of our lives, we can choose to change our experience at least to some extent. What is more we can do this faster or slower, depending on how truly we believe in our ability to jettison unhelpful associations and start afresh.

Gratitude is another key factor, especially when our lives are far from what we want them to be. Even when we're at our lowest ebb, if we can force ourselves to focus on those things we can be thankful for – even if it's only our health, or the fact we have some sort of roof over our head – it automatically switches our focus away from the negative and towards the positive.

There is one other suggestion that may help this process of change. Remember that, if you're poor, there are other versions of your life in the simulated game in which you're rich – it's just that, based on your past decisions, these versions aren't a very likely future for you as things stand. But you can change direction and attract them into your experience. The same if you're lonely – there are other possible futures in which you're surrounded by love. And so on and so forth.

The key point is that from a certain perspective these alternative, more desirable versions of your life *already exist* and don't even have to be created. That may just be the spark that allows you to believe that you really *can* change things, by selecting and fully identifying with one of your more desirable projected realities to replace the one you're currently experiencing.

there are no life plans, only the
'givens' you were born into...
so it's up to you to paint the
best picture you can
with the palette you've
been presented with

SH*T DOESN'T JUST HAPPEN!!

Let us now return to the question of the apparent inequalities between different people's lives, which we raised in an earlier chapter. We saw that the traditional reincarnation model suggests that each of us has many lives in which we experience all the extremes this realm has to offer – love and rejection, feast and famine, strength and weakness, and so on – in order that we see both sides of every coin. This is typically placed in the context that, when in soul form in the 'interlife' between each pair of lives, we review our progress and growth; also that we're involved in the planning of our next life, and the selection of its challenges. These ideas are now very much part of at least the Western reincarnation model.[17]

The problem is that if all lives are simultaneous we simply can't talk in conventional terms of growth *from* one life to the *next*, or of planning a *next* one, any more. Of course our supersoul *is* trying out a huge range of different experiences via its many projections, and its consciousness *is* expanding. But can we in any sensible way say

[17] For details see *The Big Book of the Soul*, chapter 6.

that we, as just one aspect of it, have a full awareness of this process and of all our fellow projections? Can we even talk about *our* many lives any more? The answer is only if we were genuinely able to adopt the perspective of our supersoul level of consciousness – which, while we're in human form, must be seen as extremely unlikely.

What about when we're no longer in human form? The pioneering OOB explorer Robert Monroe does describe becoming aware of and temporarily merging with some of the other aspects of his greater self during one of his journeys.[18] But, as far as souls who've genuinely departed from the earth plane are concerned, this would be a relatively advanced activity for them to engage in – one that could only occur once they'd progressed to the point where their consciousness could operate in a plane of relatively high vibration.[19] Indeed this would mark the start of gaining a more supersoul level of awareness.

[18] For details see *Supersoul*, chapter 4.
[19] The higher planes are discussed in *Afterlife*, Part 5.

SH*T DOESN'T JUST HAPPEN!!

But, as we noted in an earlier chapter, based on the OOB evidence this broadening of awareness by no means happens automatically or swiftly after death. Instead for the most part individual soul projections continue to identify with the personality of the life from which they've just departed, perhaps for some considerable 'time'.

Nevertheless, and to return to the question of inequality, it remains clear that we're each born with a set of what I've chosen to call 'birth givens', which vary enormously from one person to another and have a huge impact on our subsequent lives. These include our sex, our main psychological, emotional and physical traits, the characters of our parents and other family members, their socio-economic position and geographic location, and so on.

So, especially if we can no longer make the traditional assumption that we as an individual soul are involved in the process, who decides what our birth givens are? The answer must be, of course, our supersoul itself, which tries out myriads of unique and different combinations of these givens so they can add to their databanks of experience.

SH*T DOESN'T JUST HAPPEN!!

Indeed it's these birth givens, and all the belief systems we build on top of these as we develop through adulthood, that most condition our experience. Most people expend plenty of effort attempting to proactively direct the major decisions in their lives, especially in terms of their choice of job, home, partner and so on. But apart from this, for anyone unfamiliar with the concept of conscious creation, the rest of their experience will tend to be unconsciously determined by these underlying beliefs that are in turn significantly influenced by their birth givens.

What is more if their beliefs are sufficiently negative in any given area of their life – regarding money, or partners, or whatever – then as we've seen even their conscious desires will be thwarted, or at least their decisions and choices will turn out to be less than ideal.

In one sense this means that what we really need to concentrate on isn't the deliberate and conscious creation of certain specific outcomes in our lives, but on fostering more general attitudes and beliefs that are life-affirming, and more based on love than fear. Everything else can then flow from this, and conscious creation can be used perhaps quite sparingly for the creation of specific outcomes, and more as a bonus than as the fundamental objective. That is not to make light of the fact that, for those born with particularly disadvantageous birth givens, turning around belief systems that have always had their roots deeply embedded in fear and lack is a serious challenge.

This idea of birth givens also helps us to explain how the seemingly never-ending stream of humanitarian crises around the world dovetail with the primacy of the law of attraction. Clearly a huge number of innocent people's lives are devastated in each one, because either they or loved ones are killed in the fighting, or they're forced to flee as refugees, or they're incarcerated or enslaved, and so on. I wouldn't for one moment dare to suggest that every single one of these people has *attracted* these appalling outcomes into their lives, even subconsciously. But what *is* clear is that being born in certain geographical areas at certain times is a pretty sure guarantee of a disrupted and challenging life.

Beyond this idea of birth givens, and however much my earlier research concentrated on such things, I now believe we have to conclude there are no 'life plans', perhaps not even any over-riding 'soul purpose'. Any of these would only detract from our ability to use our free will to create whatever experience we choose, and to change our mind and recreate ourselves afresh as many times as we like.

The only exception to all this is in the area of what are commonly called 'soul contracts'. These are traditionally tied into the concept of planning a next life in conjunction with another soul and agreeing to have certain interactions with each other, often of a challenging nature. It is clear that our supersoul's selection of our parents and siblings, perhaps even extending to friends from our childhood, is very much part of our birth givens.

On that basis a pattern of interaction with any of *these*, set up during childhood but extending into our adult lives, can be seen under our new model as stemming from a birth given – but equally could still be thought of as some sort of contract. As long as, that is, we don't see this interaction as entirely predetermined, but instead as something which as adults we have complete free will to handle in whatever way we choose.

Again a personal example may be useful at this point. The person who started me off on the spiritual path was a girl called Sarah. I was in my mid-thirties and I happened to notice her in the centre of the city where I lived at the time, walking into a downstairs bar alone. I wouldn't normally follow someone in that situation but there was something about her, her jaunty walk, something that made me go after her. Within no time she was telling me we'd shared lives together in Atlantis, which to me sounded like complete nonsense. It took nearly a year of persistence on her part before I took anything she said seriously, but eventually I gave in. The relationship that followed wasn't a long-term success, but I've always been grateful to her for setting me on a path that has been my major inspiration ever since.

Using a traditional interpretation I always assumed that she and I must have had a pre-agreed soul contract that she would put me on the spiritual path, which was my true life purpose. But is there an equally satisfactory but different explanation using our new model?

Yes, I believe there is. For a start we've seen that consciousness in all its forms has a fundamental desire to expand, and we as humans achieve this in all sorts of ways – from great scientists and philosophers to the apparently humblest mothers and fathers quietly and protectively raising their children, everyone plays their part. I would argue that by a combination of birth-given traits and consciously taken decisions I happen to have tended towards spiritual philosophy.

For example, I know that from the earliest age I was fascinated by ghost stories and the like. Then in my twenties, despite my avowed atheism, I can distinctly remember being rather taken by the idea of Atlantis, and also by Erich von Däniken's *Chariots of the Gods* – whatever I might now think of his research. As a result I can remember deciding that the issue of whether or not there are extraterrestrials living on other planets was at the heart of my understanding of who I was, and was something I would need to look into more deeply when I had the time. Actually I've gone in other directions since, but I think I can safely say that deep inside I always knew there was 'something more'.

So arguably Sarah was simply someone I attracted into my life based on interests and leanings I'd already displayed. More broadly I can see that embarking on a path of spiritual research may have been partly a natural development from my birth givens, particularly a tendency towards introspection. But it was also about conscious adult decisions – for example, to end my commercial career and embark on a life of research. In particular I could easily have taken the decision not to start a writing career, or to finish it at innumerable points over the last two decades when the going got tough. But here I still am, at least for now. It has all been my choice – and I don't feel that anyone or anything has particularly influenced it except myself.

There are further implications if this analysis is correct. A significant element of the traditional reincarnation model is that we each have one or more guides or even angels whose main function is to watch over us, and particularly to keep us on our 'path'. But what if we don't have a path? Do they still exist?

My best guess would be that there may be what

are probably other projections of our supersoul who *do* keep some sort of an eye on us from other planes. But, if the law of attraction remains paramount, I'd still argue that they're unlikely to interfere in our lives any proactive way. The exceptions to this would be if we've deliberately asked for their help, which is a form of attraction in itself. Or more generally if they're simply assisting in the process of 'oiling the wheels' of how the universe brings the law of attraction into physical manifestation in the first place.

Which brings us neatly onto the whole issue of 'synchronicities'. Many people regard these as signs that the universe or our guides are keeping us on our chosen path, perhaps even nudging us back onto it if we take too much of a diversion. But under our new model, rather than being related to any life plan or path, they simply give us the opportunities to make our *own* conscious desires at any given time come true, provided we're open and aware and notice them. In other words they only represent the sophisticated underlying dynamics of how, as a human, our own ongoing creation and attraction process crystallises into our experience of the physical.

SH*T DOESN'T JUST HAPPEN!!

My meeting the girl in the hat is surely just such an example.

So what about intuition? In the past we've tended to see this as some higher aspect of ourself nudging us that something will either be good or bad for us, and again we've tended to place this in the context of being either aligned or misaligned with our life path. But under our new model we might, for example, explain it as a connection with a resonant soul who has already been through a similar experience and found it beneficial or otherwise. Additionally it could represent a seepage of information about possible futures in the simulated game – and of whether, for example, they result in a pleasurable or painful experience. Again neither of these relate to the idea of a life plan or path.

Of course we could also be receiving an intuitive nudge from our supersoul itself, but our new model suggests that in the main this would only result from our proactively asking for help. Above all, of course, we have complete free will to over-ride or ignore any of these promptings, although usually to our detriment.

All this suggests that even 'it's not meant to be'

can no longer be used as an excuse for failing to achieve a desired outcome – as philosophical as this view usually sounds. Instead the most likely explanation is that we're subconsciously sabotaging the outcome, meaning we'd be able to achieve it in time if we were to do more work on our limiting beliefs. But, more generally, if we don't have life plans so that no-one is proactively trying to guide us, and if our supersoul is broadly neutral about the experiences we're having, then the idea of something being *meant* to be or not simply has no reference point.

Nevertheless, I repeat that doesn't mean we can't proactively ask for guidance or help from our supersoul – or other aspects of it – in respect of any path we *ourselves* have chosen to take at any given time.

I have attempted to encapsulate all the above in the following sentence:

> *Each of us has to paint the best picture we can using the palette we've been given by the higher, divine aspect of ourselves.*

What is meant by 'best' picture? It involves

living life to the full with enthusiasm and joy. It means manifesting abundance in our lives in whatever way we choose to define it. It means picking ourselves up when we fall and being prepared to start all over again. It means coming as much as possible from a place of love not fear. Some will naturally be able to achieve this far more easily than others, purely because their birth givens include more favourable life circumstances and psychological propensities. But everyone – and I mean *everyone* – can strive to achieve these goals at least to some extent.

We all know of people born with superficially less favourable physical or mental traits who've gone on to act as shining examples to the rest of us – paralympians being an obvious example. We equally know of people born with huge apparent advantages who've spiralled into drug abuse and suicide. So, birth givens aside, it really is all about personal choice.

To sum up the inequality question, under our new model any particularly challenging set of birth givens might perhaps be seen as 'taking one for the team', while generally each of us can be characterised as a 'lead representative of team supersoul gaining experience at the coalface of space-time on behalf of the collective'. In fact effectively we're all acting altruistically on behalf of our supersoul.

So what practical steps can we take to improve our experience and to live with more enthusiasm and joy? There are huge numbers of self-help books available on this topic, and we cannot hope to summarise all the excellent advice available. But we've already seen that probably the simplest and most effective change we can make is to stop allowing our everyday thoughts to fixate on the things we *don't* want in our life, and to focus instead on what we *do* want. This requires patience and perseverance and will keep our observer self extremely busy. But, if rigorously applied, it'll produce huge results all by itself.

What is meant by focus? It involves putting our whole self into visualising and affirming the person we want to be, or the outcomes we want to create. It means using our imagination and emotions as much as possible to breathe life into our incipient creation. In fact those who express their belief to the maximum act as if they've *already achieved* the outcome they desire.

We have seen that a true master can alter their reality in an instant, and this means *any* of us if we have sufficient belief. However it won't hurt most of us to accept that our creations may take a little time to materialise. This means we need to stay excited and focused, yet loose, relaxed and patient. If we are over-expectant and impatient we tighten up on our dreams, our belief weakens and we let fear of *not* achieving them get in the way. We will return to this topic later.

So how high should we aim? Those starting out on the path of consciously creating the life they desire are often told to 'start small', and this may indeed be good advice. But it shouldn't blind us to the fact that, as suggested in the last chapter, the sky is pretty much the limit. This means we can create any outcome we desire, subject only to our birth givens. For example, even a true master might struggle to regrow a limb that was never there, or had been lost in an accident or through illness.

But to pick up on the objection raised in the opening chapter, it should be clear by now that even those who are currently in less favourable circumstances – whether due to their birth givens or not – have exactly the same innate capacity to create a different and more desirable life for themselves as anyone else. It may be more of a challenge, and obtaining the same results as someone starting from a more advantageous place may take longer or require more belief – which is why we should never make any sort of judgement about anyone else's attempts to change their lives, or compare their efforts with our own, because we're all different. But ultimately the same innate capacity to change our lives exists in all of us.

What is more, although this isn't intuitively obvious to our human minds, the universe makes no distinction between us wanting to manifest, say, a million pounds or just a hundred. The only difference lies in the degree of our *own* belief.

even if you don't understand
how you attracted certain
major challenges, if you assume
you must have done you take
full responsibility... especially
for your reaction to them

SH*T DOESN'T JUST HAPPEN!!

Now is a good time to remind ourselves of a few points made in the opening chapter.

First, victimhood is suffering because it places us in a position where we feel we're not in control, and at the mercy of someone or something else. That always leads to stress and hurt. By contrast it's very hard to suffer when we feel we're in control. It naturally follows that if we take full responsibility for everything we experience in our life, much of our suffering will vanish. So taking responsibility isn't a burden to be avoided – it's the ultimate in self empowerment.

Second, ascribing undesirable circumstances or experiences to past lives or life plans *can* tend to abrogate responsibility and take us into victim mode, without us even being aware of it. So perhaps it's just as well that our new model based on simultaneous lives suggests these concepts no longer make sense anyway.

All the evidence then, combined with logic itself, points to the fact that each of us is creating the entirety of our experience – although not just via our proactive thoughts and intentions, but also via our underlying beliefs, preconceptions and attitudes.

SH*T DOESN'T JUST HAPPEN!!

We saw earlier that such a bold statement will be extremely hard for some people to accept. This is particularly the case when we come to the most difficult and contentious aspect of our new model – one that books on the law of attraction often avoid. What of those apparently wonderful people who, for example, contract a serous illness or die before their time? The individuals themselves or their loved ones will understandably look at their life and insist there's no way they could've *attracted* that.

Nothing I say about this is intended to take away from the fact that at some points in our lives we all go through traumatic events that can leave deep scars – the loss of loved ones, relationship break-ups and so on. These need healing. In fact if they're not healed properly we can descend into a destructive spiral in which subconscious patterns of behaviour escalate until we wake up and realise what's happening. This *can* occur *even if* we know we're just actors in a play, and *even if* we take full responsibility for what we've created – and sometimes serious therapy of one form or another will be required because we simply can't process our grief properly by ourselves. This is especially true when, as is often the case, the trauma stems from childhood.

That having been said, to return to the idea that everything is attracted, the first thing to be aware of is that there are certain mitigations. Children for example aren't fully responsible for their lives until they grow up and achieve independence, which happens at a different time for each of us. So any major challenges they face will form part of their birth givens, rather than being something they've attracted into their lives.

In addition I can only conclude that our supersoul consciousness *might* occasionally present us with additional challenges as an adult. This could be because it feels we can handle them as an additional part of our experience; perhaps even because we've done better than expected in learning how to cope with those challenges we've already faced related to our birth givens. This might seem to detract from the primacy of our free will, but arguably it's not so different from being allocated a certain set of givens at the outset. It would just be another way for our supersoul to vary our collective experience.

SH*T DOESN'T JUST HAPPEN!!

This would mean these new challenges *weren't* something we'd attracted, at least not in the conventional sense. But I'd suggest that we should aim to regard such *un*attracted challenges as a rare occurrence, certainly to the extent that we're considering their possible existence in our own life. Otherwise, again, we can tend to lapse into victimhood.

By contrast it might make us feel better to use this as an explanation for the experiences of others, especially those close to us. But we'd also do well to remember that, however things look from the outside, we never really know what conflicts lie deep inside someone else's psyche. Indeed we're often blissfully unaware of what's going on deep within our own until we learn to look. When we're considering severe illness or premature death, it's also worth noting Seth's view that people project their deepest inner conflicts into different areas. Different people can manifest the same basic conflict in, for example, poverty, or in loneliness, or in ill-health. No two people are the same.

In any case the most important aspect of all this, of course, is how we *react* to any new challenges. Irrespective of whether we consider them to have been introduced into our lives by our supersoul, or to have been attracted entirely by ourselves, what we can definitely control and take full responsibility for is how we respond. Is it with love, or fear? *This* is what really matters.

In this respect again we've seen how brave paralympians who've been injured in terrorist attacks, conflicts or accidents have set shining examples of how to react to adversity. Many have picked themselves up and created lives that they perceive to be even more rewarding and exciting than before they were injured. Understandably they might have needed some time to come to terms with their new situation, and might even have lapsed into initial victimhood. But what they all share is how they pulled themselves around and started afresh.

life isn't about suffering or mere acceptance... you expand your supersoul's consciousness far more if you aim for joyful abundance and to fulfil your maximum potential

SH*T DOESN'T JUST HAPPEN!!

Certain spiritual approaches, typically with their origins in the East, revolve around concepts such as *trusting*, *allowing*, *accepting*, *surrendering* and *flowing*. Most often this involves a completely different context from the one we've been considering – one in which the idea of setting ourselves specific goals, even of having any involvement in creating our own reality at all, is anathema.

Of course I'm generalising massively, but such worldviews tend to assume that whatever consciousness underlies the universe directs everything, and that to attempt to consciously interfere with its plans is to mistakenly allow the ego to try to meddle with the divine process. The corollary is that any proactive action of that nature may well see us swimming against the tide. So the advice seems to be just to sit back, relax and let the divine universe get on with organising things for us.

Such a path of least resistance can, of course, appear hugely attractive. I would even go as far as to suggest that the very words *acceptance* and *flow* have an automatic connotation of wisdom and serenity. But is following such a path quite as desirable as it might at first appear? Take someone whose birth givens were so challenging that they've been unable to overcome them and have ended up homeless and living on the street, leading a wretched, miserable life of dependence and victimhood. This is as good an example of total surrender as I can think of – but can it really be said to be working well for such people?

In a previous chapter we discussed the importance of creating positive belief systems generally, and once we do that there's an extent to which we can just *surrender* and *flow* because we've done the hard work. But this approach still accepts the huge creative power each of us has as an individual aspect of our supersoul, as opposed to assuming that some sort of universal consciousness we can't possibly fathom lies behind the process. Of course just like any belief system this latter approach will produce a set of choices and experiences that add to our supersoul's databanks. But is it the enlightened choice it might at first appear? Indeed is it one that will help humanity as a whole to evolve into its full creative power? It seems not.

More specifically, though, the commonplace advice when we're attempting to consciously create in specific areas of our lives is to concentrate on the *what* of the outcome, but not on exactly *how* it will be achieved. In other words having set the outcome we desire, and while holding that firmly in view, we must make sure we don't sabotage it by trying to dictate the specifics of *how* it's brought about. Otherwise we restrict the freedom of the universal creation process to bring our desired outcome to fruition. This is again where ideas of *surrender*, of *flow*, of *trust* and of *allowing* become relevant.

This is when we'd be in danger of going against the flow, and of upsetting the complex underlying dynamics of how the universe manifests our true desires. It may be trying to produce an outcome in one way but, if we're putting all our focus into trying to force it to occur in a different way, that's bound to mess things up.

As a simple example let's say that we want to manifest a new partner. If we're not being sufficiently patient with the creation process we might put all our focus into one person who happens to attract us and who's in our life now, while the person who's really far more in line with our true desires has yet to make an appearance. This misguided focus might even prevent that person from appearing at all or, when they do, we might miss the opportunity because we're already committed elsewhere.

Having said which it's probably worth considering the fact that some people *do* manage to create the outcome they desire by being absolutely fastidious about exactly *how* it will be brought about, and nowhere is there a better example than, again, that of the sporting world. Top level sportspeople – Formula One teams, for example – only reach the pinnacle by being meticulous in trying to control every single variable, and in doing that better than the others. If you told them to just 'go with the flow' and 'trust' they would laugh.

But we should be clear that this is an exception to the rule. Of course we could follow their example in our own lives, but it would involve huge amounts of hard work and might still end in failure. Whereas setting the goal, then holding it in focus with determination and belief but at the same time stepping back and letting the manifestation process flow, is surely a far easier approach.

This doesn't mean sitting back and doing nothing at all, however. We should always be prepared to take action when inspired. That very inspiration itself will, if we're properly in tune, be the universe prompting us that this is something that will help us achieve our goal.

We can summarise all this in the following advice:

> *Focus on the outcomes you desire and take action when inspired, but don't keep constantly striving to make them happen from moment to moment.*

For some people another major objection to the law of attraction generally is they perceive the pursuit of abundance as incompatible with adopting a loving approach to life. This may or may not be a reflection of the fact that, to many orthodox religious worldviews, the idea that we're having this experience to actually *enjoy* it is anathema. But actually the two aren't in conflict at all. In fact aiming for abundance, however each of us might define it, is the only way to consistently come from a place of love not fear – meaning we expand our supersoul's consciousness as much as possible. On the face of it this sounds counterintuitive, so let's find out why.

First, our shared experience with the rest of humanity is *not* a competition, however much it might appear that way when we look, for example, at the apparent inequalities of resources and opportunities around the globe. Again it might seem counterintuitive but the clear consensus from the OOB and channelled evidence I've consulted suggests that our individual and collective desires have the ability to manifest unlimited joyful abundance for *everyone*, because that's how our reality works – if only we'd learn to use it in the right way. So if we're creating abundance for ourselves it doesn't *have* to mean we're taking it away from someone else – although we may well be if we're motivated by a desire to control and compete, and by fear of loss and selfishness. It all depends what our underlying intentions are.

Second, the goal of creating joyful abundance for ourselves can of course be expressed in many different ways. Some people may want to pursue what others would deride as unduly materialistic aims – such as having more money, a bigger house or a better body. But these are absolutely fine as long as they bring genuine happiness and joy to those who pursue them, and to the people around them. That is why the key is *joyful* abundance – because all too often the pursuit of purely materialist aims brings no joy, only an eternally unfulfilled yearning for more.

So we should be ever wary of judging the choices that others make. We should also remind ourselves that there's no one in a position of supposed authority, in any realm, who'll judge us for whatever way we choose to manifest abundance in our lives. Again the only rider to this is that if at the same time we cause harm to someone else, especially knowingly and deliberately, our actions are no longer entirely love-based and expansive.

Nevertheless others may find happiness in quite different ways, such as pursuing hobbies or sports and so on, and often these are indeed far more joyful and fulfilling than purely materialistic aims. Moreover, precisely because love is such a strong motivator in this reality we're experiencing, some people feel strongly drawn to putting others before themselves –

and *this* is their main source of joy. They might simply devote themselves to their family, or to their local community, or even to the wider global community in some way.

We should be in no doubt that service to others is a truly noble and loving ideal. However even this comes with several health warnings. First, any sense of superiority that arises from the choice of such a path doesn't come from a place of love. Second, helping others with joy, not as a duty, is the only way to truly express love for them – otherwise there's a tendency towards martyrdom and victimhood. Third, it's sad to say that often those who concentrate on global issues such as the environment are initially motivated by love and altruism, but they can end up being consumed by fear and anger – and over time this is likely to have a seriously detrimental effect on them personally.

*the next major step in human
evolution, and the aim of the
shift in consciousness... is to
appreciate that we are the
creator gods of myth and legend*

SH*T DOESN'T JUST HAPPEN!!

Some of our wisest channelled sources are quite forthright in suggesting that it's time for the human race to let go of simplistic notions that any number of gods or prophets, or our karma or life plans, are dictating what we experience. However comforting these ideas might seem, perhaps it's time for us to move towards a more evolved and empowered spiritual worldview.

If there is a major shift in human consciousness occurring at the moment, and many people believe there is, then I'd argue that more than anything it involves us finally understanding that we each create our reality in its entirety – and that we should learn to do this consciously and deliberately.

We don't have to work miracles or move mountains, although we can if we choose and have sufficient belief. The people we most admire are those who follow their dreams despite all the apparent evidence that they're not achievable. Those who conquer apparently insurmountable odds. These are the people who simply refuse to react to their environment or situation using conventional belief systems, and create different, seemingly impossible ones – then over time, with a resolute and steely determination and sense of purpose, bring them to fruition.

On the other hand, simply taking control of our lives and fashioning them in whatever way suits us, making big changes or small, and doing this whenever we want and however many times we want – *that* will be a major step forward. In fact even if we only manage partial control while we're learning the ropes, this is far better than having no control at all. Indeed just recognising that we have control in the first place, whether we use it consciously or not, is a huge step forward for any individual.

Do we still need to strive for 'ascension' or 'enlightenment', as so many spiritual approaches suggest? Or is this in truth just spiritual ego in action? If so, is there another way? I would humbly suggest there is.

> *Simply recognising that you're the master of your own creation is all you need to do to reconnect with your true divinity.*

This is surely the next major step in human evolution. Greater, perhaps, than any other. The potential is there for us to stop using our brains in the reactive, survival mode that served us so well when we needed to be constantly on the lookout for danger. Instead we can learn to depend far less on past associations, and to switch into a more proactive, creative mode in which we're living in the present and constructing new associations as it suits us.

Both individually and collectively, the potential is there for us to make our dreams come true. Each of us can make a start until at some point the collective will creates an unstoppable tide. Without any formal efforts at conversion or persuasion, eventually a new spiritual enlightenment based on total personal responsibility will surely sweep away the superstition of more traditional approaches. While in due course fundamentalist materialism will surely come to be seen as a blinkered anachronism that no longer fits the available evidence.

Now that's a future for humanity to look forward to.

Are you ready to play your part?

the ten principles of
'Supersoul Spirituality'

SH*T DOESN'T JUST HAPPEN!!

This summary is taken from chapter 7 of *Supersoul*:

1. We are multidimensional, expeditionary soul probes sent out by a supersoul consciousness possessing a wisdom and power of divine proportions. Myriad supersouls are involved in the simulation game we call 'human life on earth', which is just one of myriad different realities soul probes are sent into.

2. After death we continue to identify with the personality of the life we just left, so this and the 'soul' are the same consciousness.

3. Although we're still engaged in the growth of consciousness, we don't develop in a linear fashion as we move from one reincarnatory life to another. Instead the lives of all soul probes projected by the supersoul are happening at the same time – even if they're operating in different human eras – and they interact as a complex matrix. By logic alone this means the 'interlife' is only an *after*life, and possibly a *pre*life too.

4. 'My' many lives means nothing unless we're genuinely adopting our supersoul level of

consciousness, which involves appreciating that we're far more powerful and multi-faceted than we normally recognise. Any experiences we have of 'past' or 'future' lives are most likely those of other 'resonant souls' from our supersoul with whom we have an especially close connection – for example because of strongly shared traits or challenges, or because they act as contrasts.

5. Each of us is fundamentally responsible for creating our own experience in each moment of now. We're not limited by 'past karma' from this life or a supposedly previous one unless we believe we are. Nor will other resonant souls tend to be able to exert a strongly disruptive influence over us unless we believe they can and choose to let them.

6. Our supersoul chooses our 'birth givens', and these vary considerably. They include our own sex, our main psychological and physical traits and propensities – in terms of both challenges and strengths – and the socio-economic position and geographical location of our parents. On that basis we're here to 'paint the best picture we can with

the palette we've been given'. Other than that any pre-birth planning of events in our adult lives, or 'soul contracts' with others, are probably kept to a minimum to give us maximum free will to direct our experience. It's also unlikely that most of us have a preplanned 'life purpose', because again this would tend to detract from our free will to follow whatever purpose we desire – and to change that purpose, should we so choose, at any time.

7. Angels and guides may well be other aspects of our own supersoul, and they won't tend to interfere with our experience on the basis that they supposedly 'know best' and 'want to keep us on our path'. Usually therefore synchronicities will only represent the sophisticated underlying dynamics of how our *own* creation and attraction process crystallises into our experience of the physical.

8. Having said that, insights and guidance are always available if we *proactively* ask for them, or if we *attract* them to ourselves automatically by our conscious intentions and actions. Such guidance might come, for

example, from wiser, non-incarnate aspects of our supersoul consciousness, or from other resonant souls who've overcome similar challenges. We can also provide guidance to them by overcoming our own challenges, if they're open to it.

9. On rare occasions we might make a new agreement with our supersoul, at a subconscious level, to take on a new challenge in our adult lives. But it's always best to take responsibility for any challenge by assuming you created or attracted it, or at least by knowing you control your reaction to it. Any tendency to ascribe challenges to 'past' karma, life plans or soul contracts can lead to an abrogation of responsibility for what we're creating in the now, and detract from our extensive power to turn any situation around.

10. Under a matrix model *everything* can be seen as altruistic, because everything that each soul experiences is designed to add to the databanks of the supersoul consciousness. Any particularly challenging circumstances or birth givens can best be seen in the context of 'taking one for the

team', and each of us can be characterised as a 'lead representative of team supersoul gaining experience at the coalface of space-time on behalf of the collective'.

appendix

The main pioneering OOB explorers quoted in *Afterlife* are as follows:

- Aardema, Frederick, *Explorations in Consciousness* (Mount Royal Publishing, 2012).

- Besant, Annie, *Ancient Wisdom* (Kessinger Publishing, 1998).

- Buhlman, William, *Adventures Beyond the Body* and *The Secret of the Soul* (HarperOne, 1996/2001) and *Adventures in the Afterlife* (CreateSpace, 2013).

- Dack, Graham, *The Out-of-Body Experience* (OOBEX Publishing, 1999).

- Fox, Oliver (Hugh Callaway), *Astral Projection* (Citadel Press, 1962).

- Larsen, Caroline, *My Travels in the Spirit World* (Tuttle, 1927).

- Leadbeater, Charles Webster, *The Devachanic Plane* (Theosophical Publishing House, 1974) and *The Astral Plane* (Theosophical Publishing Society, 1895).

- McKnight, Rosalind, *Cosmic Journeys* and

Soul Journeys (Hampton Roads, 1999/2005).

- Moen, Bruce, *Voyage into the Unknown*, *Voyage Beyond Doubt*, *Voyages into the Afterlife* and *Voyage to Curiosity's Father* (Hampton Roads, 1997/1998/1999/2001).

- Monroe, Robert, *Journeys Out of the Body*, *Far Journeys* and *Ultimate Journey* (Broadway Books, 2001).

- Morrell, Ed, *The Twenty-Fifth Man* (New Era Publishing, 1924).

- Phinn, Gordon, *Eternal Life and How To Enjoy It* (Hampton Roads, 2004), *More Adventures in Eternity* (O Books, 2008) and *You Are History* (White Crow Books, 2015).

- Sculthorp, Frederick, *Excursions to the Spirit World* (Greater World Association, 1969).

- Swedenborg, Emanuel, *Heaven and Hell* (Swedenborg Foundation, 2009).

- Taylor, Albert, *Soul Traveller* (New American Library, 2000).

- Twitchell, Paul, *Eckankar: The Key to Secret Worlds* (Illuminated Way Publishing, 1987).

- Turvey, Vincent, *The Beginnings of Seership* (University Books, 1969).

- Van Dam, Vee, *The Psychic Explorer* (Skoob Books, 1989).
- Vieira, Waldo, *Projections of the Consciousness* (International Academy of Consciousness, 2007).
- 'Yram' (Marcel Forhan), *Practical Astral Projection* (Samuel Weiser, 1974).
- Ziewe, Jurgen, *Multidimensional Man* (Lulu.com, 2008).

The channelled sources quoted in *The Power of You* are as follows:

- 258 lectures by the Pathwork Guide, channelled by Eva Pierrakos from 1957 to 1979 (see *www.pathwork.org/the-lectures*).
- Seth channelled by Jane Roberts from 1963 to 1984, especially in *Seth Speaks* and *The Nature of Personal Reality* (Amber-Allen, 1994).
- Ramtha channelled by JZ Knight from 1979, especially in *The White Book* (JZK Publishing, 2004).
- Bashar channelled by Darryl Anka from 1983 (see *www.bashar.org/fundamentals.html*).

SH*T DOESN'T JUST HAPPEN!!

- Abraham channelled by Esther Hicks from 1988, especially in *The Law of Attraction* (Hay House, 2007).

- 'God' channelled by Neale Donald Walsch from 1991 in *Conversation with God: Books 1-3* (Hodder and Stoughton, 1997-9).

- Jeshua channelled by Jayem (Jon Marc Hammer) from 1994 in *The Way of Mastery* (Heartfelt Publishing PMA, 1995).

- Elias channelled by Mary Ennis from 1995 (see *www.eliasforum.org/transcripts.html*).

the Supersoul Series

all published by Rational Spirituality Press
see *www.rspress.org* and *www.ianlawton.com*

RESEARCH BOOKS

[Volume 1] SUPERSOUL (2013) is the main reference book for Supersoul Spirituality, containing out-of-body and channelled evidence that each and every one of us is a holographic reflection of a supersoul that has power way beyond our wildest imaginings.

[Volume 2] THE POWER OF YOU (2014) compares modern channelled wisdom from a variety of well-known sources, all emphasising that each of us is consciously or unconsciously creating every aspect of our own reality, and that this is what the current consciousness shift is all about.

[Volume 3] AFTERLIFE (2019) is a state-of-the-art, clear, reliable guide to the afterlife based on the underlying consistencies in traditional channelled material and modern out-of-body research.

SH*T DOESN'T JUST HAPPEN!! (2016) introduces Supersoul Spirituality by explaining how and why we ourselves create or attract everything we experience in our adult lives... so that we are never victims of chance, God's will, our karma or our life plans.

WHAT JESUS WAS REALLY SAYING (2016) is a fundamental reinterpretation of the Christian message that uses excerpts from the Gospels to propose that, through his supposed miracles, Jesus was trying to show us that each of us is a creator god of the highest order and can manipulate the illusion we call reality at will.

THE GOD WHO SOMETIMES SCREWED UP (2018) charts the author's progression from motorcycle and car racer, to pyramid explorer and researcher of ancient civilisations, to spiritual philosopher... with analysis and examples of how he has created or manifested all the various aspects of his life, both good and bad.

DEATH SHOULD BE FUN!! (2019) is a light-hearted look at the afterlife, concentrating on the unlimited possibilities we have to create wondrous new experiences in the higher planes of consciousness... as long as we have a map of the territory, and we're aware that we're in control and that the sky's the limit.

IAN LAWTON was born in 1959. Formerly an accountant, sales exec, business and IT consultant and avid bike and car racer, in his mid-thirties he changed tack completely to become a writer-researcher specialising in ancient history and, more recently, spiritual philosophy. His first two books, *Giza: The Truth* and *Genesis Unveiled*, sold over 30,000 copies worldwide.

In his *Books of the Soul Series* he originated the ideas of Rational Spirituality and of the holographic soul. But since 2013 he has been developing the more radical worldview of Supersoul Spirituality in the *Supersoul Series*. A short film clip discussing the latter can be found at *www.ianlawton.com* and on YouTube.